For Ma

For Mother With Love

THE TRUEST FRIEND WE HAVE

COMPILED BY

SARAH ANNE STUART

BRISTOL PARK BOOKS

The acknowledgements on pages 125 to 126
constitute an extension of the copyright page.

First Bristol Park Books edition published
in 2014

Bristol Park Books
252 W. 38th Street
NYC, NY 10018

Bristol Park Books is a registered trademark
of Bristol Park Books, Inc.

Library of Congress Control Number
2013956261

ISBN: 978-0-88486-553-7

Text and cover designed by Cindy LaBreacht

Printed in the United States of America

Contents

Introduction

From our infancy and through the pain and pleasure of learning and growing, each of us has a mother—be it our birth mother or that special caring person whom we love and who loved us—who oversaw our growth to full adulthood. These selected poems and perceptive observations from voices as varied as Robert Louis Stevenson, Phyllis McGinley, William Wordsworth, Abraham Lincoln, and Oscar Wilde celebrate the gift of motherhood.

It is hoped that this collection can be a 'thank you' to all the mothers whose everlasting love gave courage to their offspring as they faced an uncertain and inconstant world.

SARAH ANNE STUART

Nurturing

A mother's arms are made
of tenderness and children
sleep soundly in them.

VICTOR HUGO

A MAN'S WORK is from sun to sun,
but a mother's work is never done.

AUTHOR UNKNOWN

Mother's Hands

Dear gentle hands have stroked my hair
    And cooled my brow,
Soft hands that pressed me close
    And seemed to know somehow
Those fleeting moods and erring thoughts
    That cloud my day,
Which quickly melt beneath their suffrage
    And pass away.

No other balm for earthly pain
    Is half so sure,
No sweet caress so filled with love
    Nor half so pure,
No other soul so close akin that understands,
No touch that brings such perfect peace as
        Mother's hands.

W. DAYTON WEDGEFARTH

The Mother's Hymn

Lord who ordainst for mankind
Benignant toils and tender cares,
We thank thee for the ties that bind
The mother to the child she bears.

We thank thee for the hopes that rise
Within her heart, as, day by day,
The dawning soul, from those young eyes,
Looks with a clearer, steadier ray.

And grateful for the blessing given
With that dear infant on her knee,
She trains the eye to look to heaven,
The voice to lisp a prayer to Thee.

Such thanks the blessed Mary gave
When from her lap the Holy Child,
Sent from on high to seek and save
The lost of earth, looked up and smiled.

All-Gracious! Grant to those who bear
A mother's charge, the strength and light
To guide the feet that own their care
In ways of Love and Truth and Right.

WILLIAM CULLEN BRYANT

Nobody Knows But Mother

How many buttons are missing today?
    Nobody knows but Mother.
How many playthings are strewn in her way?
    Nobody knows but Mother.
How many thimbles and spools has she missed?
How many burns on each fat little fist?
How many bumps to be cuddled and kissed?
    Nobody knows but Mother.

How many hats has she hunted today?
    Nobody knows but Mother.
Carelessly hiding themselves in the hay—
    Nobody knows but Mother.
How many handkerchiefs wilfully strayed?
How many ribbons for each little maid?
How for her care can a mother be paid?
    Nobody knows but Mother.

How many muddy shoes all in a row?
    Nobody knows but Mother.
How many stockings to darn, do you know?
    Nobody knows but Mother.
How many little torn aprons to mend?

How many hours of toil must she spend?
What is the time when her day's work shall end?
    Nobody knows but Mother.

How many lunches for Tommy and Sam?
    Nobody knows but Mother.
Cookies and apples and blackberry jam—
    Nobody knows but Mother.
Nourishing dainties for every "sweet tooth,"
Toddling Dottie or dignified Ruth—
How much love sweetens the labor, forsooth?
    Nobody knows but Mother.

How many cares does a mother's heart know?
    Nobody knows but Mother.
How many joys from her mother love flow?
    Nobody knows but Mother.
How many prayers for each little white bed?
How many tears for her babes has she shed?
How many kisses for each curly head?
    Nobody knows but Mother.

MARY MORRISON

Cradle Song

Sleep, sleep beauty bright,
Dreaming in the joys of night;
Sleep, sleep; in thy sleep
Little sorrows sit and weep.

Sweet babe, in thy face
Soft desires I can trace
Secret joys and secret smiles,
Little pretty infant wiles.

As thy softest limbs I feel
Smiles as of the morning steal
O'er thy cheek, and o'er thy breast
Where thy little heart doth rest.

O the cunning wiles that creep
In thy little heart asleep!
When thy little heart doth wake,
Then the dreadful night shall break.

WILLIAM BLAKE

Edgar A. Guest Considers "The Good Old Woman Who Lived in a Shoe" and the Good Old Truths Simultaneously

It takes a heap o' children to make a home
    that's true,
And home can be a palace grand or just a
    plain, old shoe;
But if it has a mother dear and a good old
    dad or two,
Why that's the sort of good old home for
    good old me and you.
Of all the institutions this side the Vale of
    Rest
Howe'er it be it seems to me a good old
    mother's best;
And fathers are a blessing, too, they give
    the place a tone;
In fact each child should try to have some
    parents of his own.
The food can be quite simple; just a sop of
    milk and bread
Are plenty when the kiddies know it's time
    to go to bed.

And every little sleepy-head will dream
    about the day
When he can go to work because a Man's
    Work is his Play.
And, oh, how sweet his life will seem,
    with nought to make him cross,
And he will never watch the clock and
    always mind the boss.
And when he thinks (as may occur),
    this thought will please him best:
That ninety million think the same-including
    Eddie Guest.

LOUIS UNTERMEYER

NO PAINTER'S BRUSH, nor poet's pen,
In justice to her fame,
Has ever reached half high enough
To write a mother's name.

AUTHOR UNKNOWN

Becoming a Dad

Old women say that men don't know
The pain through which all mothers go,
And maybe that is true, and yet
I vow I never shall forget
The night he came, I suffered, too,
Those bleak and dreary long hours through;
I paced the floor and mopped my brow
And waited for his glad wee-ow!
I went upstairs and then came down,
Because I saw the doctor frown
And knew beyond the slightest doubt
He wished to goodness I'd clear out.

I walked into the yard for air
And back again to hear her there,
And met the nurse, as calm as though
My world was not in deepest woe,
And when I questioned, seeking speech
Of consolation that would reach
Into my soul and strengthen me
For dreary hours that were to be:
"Progressing nicely!" that was all
She said and tip-toed down the hall;
"Progressing nicely!" nothing more,
And left me there to pace the floor.

And once the nurse came out in haste
For something that had been misplaced,
And I that had been growing bold
Then felt my blood grow icy cold;
And fear's stern chill swept over me,
I stood and watched and tried to see
Just what it was she came to get.
I haven't learned that secret yet.
I half-believe that nurse in white
Was adding fuel to my fright
And taking an unholy glee,
From time to time, in torturing me.

Then silence! To her room I crept
And was informed the doctor slept!
The doctor slept! Oh, vicious thought,
While she at death's door bravely fought
And suffered untold anguish deep,
The doctor lulled himself to sleep.
I looked and saw him stretched out flat
And could have killed the man for that.
Then morning broke, and oh, the joy:
With dawn there came to us our boy
And in a glorious little while
I went in there and saw her smile!

I must have looked a human wreck,
My collar wilted at my neck,
My hair awry, my features drawn
With all the suffering I had borne.
She looked at me and softly said,
"If I were you, I'd go to bed."
Her's was the bitterer part, I know;
She traveled through the vale of woe.
But now when women folks recall
The pain and anguish of it all
I answer them in manner sad:
"It's no cinch to become a dad."

EDGAR A. GUEST

MY MOTHER had a slender, small body,
but a large heart—a heart so large that
everybody's joys found welcome in it,
and hospitable accommodation.

MARK TWAIN

Home from the Daisied Meadows

Home from the daisied meadows, where you
        linger yet—
Home, golden-headed playmate, ere the sun
        is set.
For the dews are falling fast
And the night has come at last.
Home with you, home and lay your little head
        at rest,
Safe, safe, my little darling, on your mother's
        breast.
Lullaby, darling; your mother is watching you;
    She'll be your guardian and shield.
Lullaby, slumber, my darling, till morning be
    Bright upon mountain and field.
Long, long the shadows fall.
All white and smooth at home your little bed
        is laid
All round your head be angels.

ROBERT LOUIS STEVENSON

MOTHER'S LOVE grows by giving.

CHARLES LAMB

The Divine Office of the Kitchen
"GOD WALKS AMONG THE POTS AND PIPKINS."
—ST. TERESA

Lord of the pots and pipkins, since I have no
    time to be
A saint by doing lovely things and vigiling with
    Thee,
By watching in the twilight dawn, and
    storming Heaven's gates,
Make me a saint by getting meals, and
    washing up the plates!

Lord of the pots and pipkins, please, I offer
    Thee my souls,
The tiresomeness of tea leaves, and the
    sticky porridge bowls!
Remind me of the things I need, not just to
    save the stairs,
But so that I may perfectly lay tables into
    prayers.

Accept my roughened hands because I made
    them so for Thee!
Pretend my dishmop is a bow, which
    heavenly harmony

Makes on a fiddle frying pan; it is so hard to
    clean,
And, ah, so horrid! Hear, dear Lord, the music
    that I mean!

Although I must have Martha hands, I have a
    Mary mind,
And when I black the boots, I try Thy sandals,
    Lord, to find.
I think of how they trod our earth, what time I
    scrub the floor.
Accept this meditation when I haven't time
    for more!

Vespers and Compline come to pass by
    washing supper things.
And, mostly I am very tired; and all the heart
    that sings
About the morning's work, is gone, before me
    into bed.
Lend me, dear Lord, Thy Tireless Heart to
    work in me instead!

My matins are said overnight to praise and
    bless Thy Name
Beforehand for tomorrow's work, which will
    be just the same;
So that it seems I go to bed still in my
    working dress.
Lord make The Cinderella soon a heavenly
    Princess.

Warm all the kitchen with Thy Love and light
    it with Thy Peace!
Forgive the worrying, and make the
    grumbling words to cease.
Lord, who laid Breakfast on the shore, forgive
    the world which saith
"Can any good thing come to God out of
    poor Nazareth?"

CECILY HALLACK

The Mother's Return

A month, sweet little ones, is past
Since your dear Mother went away,—
And she tomorrow will return;
Tomorrow is the happy day.

O blessed tidings! Thought of joy!
The eldest heard with steady glee;
Silent he stood; then laughed amain—
And shouted, "Mother, come to me!"

Louder and louder did he shout,
With witless hope to bring her near,
"Nay, patience, patience, little boy!
Your tender mother cannot hear."

I told of hills, and far-off towns,
And long, long vales to travel through;—
He listens, puzzled, sore perplexed,
But he submits; what can he do?

No strife disturbs his sister's breast;
She wars not with the mystery
Of time and distance, night and day;
The bonds of our humanity.

Her joy is like an instinct, joy
Of kitten, bird, or summer fly;
She dances, runs without an aim,
She chatters in her ecstasy.

Her brother now takes up the note,
And echoes back his sister's glee;
They hug the infant in my arms,
As if to force his sympathy.

Then, settling into fond discourse,
We rested in the garden bower;
While sweetly shone the evening sun
In his departing hour.

We told o'er all that we had done,—
Our rambles by the swift brook's side
Far as the willow-skirted pool,
Where two swans together glide.

We talked of change, of winter gone,
Of green leaves on the hawthorne spray,
Of birds that build their nests and sing,
And all, "since Mother went away!"

To her these tales they will repeat,
To her our new-born tribes will show,
The goslings green, the ass's colt,
The lambs that in the meadow go.

—But see, the evening star comes forth!
To bed the children must depart;
A moment's heaviness they feel.
A sadness at the heart;

'Tis gone—and in a merry fit
They run upstairs in gamesome race;
I, too, infected by their mood,
I could have joined the wanton chase.

Five minutes pass—and, O the change!
Asleep upon their beds they lie;
Their busy limbs in perfect rest,
And closed the sparkling eye.

DOROTHY WORDSWORTH

From The Children's Hour

Between the dark and the daylight,
When the light is beginning to lower,
Comes a pause in the day's occupations
That is known as the Children's Hour.

I hear in the chamber above me
The patter of little feet,
The sound of a door that is opened,
And voices soft and sweet.

From my study I see in the lamplight,
Descending the broad hall stair,
Grave Alice and laughing Allegra,
And Edith with golden hair.

A whisper and then a silence;
Yet I know by their merry eyes,
They are plotting and planning together
To take me by surprise.

A sudden rush from the stairway,
A sudden raid from the hall!
By three doors left unguarded
They enter my castle wall!

They climb up into my turret,
O'er the arms and back of my chair;
If I try to escape they surround me;
They seem to be everywhere.

Do you think, O blue-eyed banditti,
Because you have scaled the wall,
Such an old person as I am
Is not a match for you all?

I have you fast in my fortress,
And will not let you depart,
But put you down into the dungeon
In the round-tower of my heart.

And there will I keep you forever,
Yes, forever and a day,
Till the wall shall crumble to ruin,
And moulder in dust away.

HENRY WADSWORTH LONGFELLOW

At Day's End

I hold you in my arms before the fire
And tell the fairy tale you love the best,
While winter twilight deepens and the first
White star comes forth to glitter in the west.

So softly do you lie against my heart
I scarcely know if it be child or flower
I cradle, till you stir and draw a breath
Of wonder at the tale. O, blessed hour

That every mother knows when at day's end
She holds her little child, a wistful ache
Commingling with her joy, and dreams a dream
For him and breathes a prayer for his dear sake!

ADELAIDE LOVE

GOD could not be everywhere, so he created
mothers.

JEWISH PROVERB

Upon Her Soothing Breast

Upon her soothing breast
She lulled her little child;
A winter sunset in the west,
A dreary glory smiled.

EMILY BRONTE

A Child's Grace

Here a little child I stand
Heaving up my either hand;
Cold as paddocks though they be,
Here I lift them up to Thee,
For a benison to fall
On our meat and on us all. Amen

ROBERT HERRICK

Good-night

Then the bright lamp is carried in,
The sunless hours again begin;
O'er all without, in field and lane,
The haunted night returns again.

Now we behold the embers fire
About the firelit hearth, and see
Our faces painted as we pass,
Like pictures, on the window glass.

Must we to bed indeed? Well then,
Let us arise and go like men,
And face the undaunted tread
The long black passage up to bed.

Farewell, O brother, sister, sire!
O pleasant party round the fire!
The song you sing, the tales you tell,
Till far to-morrow, fare you well!

ROBERT LOUIS STEVENSON

Child's Evening Hymn

Now the day is over,
    Night is drawing nigh,
Shadows of the evening
    Steal across the sky.

Now the darkness gathers,
    Stars begin to peep,
Birds and beasts and flowers
    Soon will be asleep.

Jesus give the weary
    Calm and sweet repose,
With they tenderest blessing
    May our eyelids close.

Grant to little children
    Visions bright of thee,
Guard the sailors tossing
    On the deep blue sea.

Comfort every sufferer
    Watching late in pain;
Those who plan some evil
    From their sin restrain.

Through the long night-watches
    May thy angels spread
Their white wings above me,
    Watching round my bed.

When the morning wakens,
    Then may I arise
Pure and fresh and sinless
    In thy holy eyes.

SABINE BARING-GOULD

SOME MOTHERS are kissing mothers
and some are scolding mothers,
but it is love just the same, and most
mothers kiss and scold together.

PEARL S. BUCK

Lullaby

Lullaby and goodnight!
With roses bedight;
Creep into thy bed,
There pillow thy head.
If God will, thou shalt wake
When the morning doth break,
If God will, thou shalt wake,
When the morning doth break.

Lullaby and goodnight;
Those blue eyes close tight;
Bright angels are near,
So sleep without fear.
They will guard thee from harm
With fair dreamland's charm,
They will guard thee from harm
With fair dreamland's charm.

JOHANNES BRAHMS

MOTHER is a verb, not a noun.

PROVERB

A MOM'S hug lasts long after
she lets go.

AUTHOR UNKNOWN

A Cradle Song

The angels are stooping
Above your bed;
They weary of trooping
With the whimpering dead.

God's laughing in heaven
To see you so good;
The Shining Seven
Are gay with his mood.

I kiss you and kiss you,
My pigeon, my own;
Ah, how I shall miss you
When you have grown.

WILLIAM BUTLER YEATS

Sweet and Low

Sweet and low, sweet and low,
Wind of the western sea;
Low, low, breathe and blow,
Wind of the western sea;
Over the rolling water go,
Come from the dying moon and blow,
Blow him again to me,
While my little one,
While my pretty one sleeps.

Sleep and rest, sleep and rest,
Father will come to thee soon;
Rest, rest on Mother's breast,
Father will come to thee soon.
Father will come to his babe in the nest,
Silver sails all out of the west,
Under the silvery moon;
Sleep, my little one,
Sleep, my pretty one, sleep.

ALFRED, LORD TENNYSON

All Through the Night

Sleep my child and peace attend thee,
All through the night;
Guardian angels God will send thee,
All through the night.
Soft the drowsy hours are creeping,
Hill and vale in slumber sleeping,
I my loving vigil keeping,
All through the night.

While the moon her watch is keeping,
All through the night;
While the weary world is sleeping,
All through the night.
O'er thy spirit gently stealing,
Visions of delight revealing,
Breathes a pure and holy feeling,
All through the night.

WELSH FOLK LULLABY

ALL MOTHERS are working mothers.

AUTHOR UNKNOWN

Teaching

That best academy,
a mother's knee.

JAMES RUSSELL LOWELL

A Mother's Prayer

Lord Jesus, You who bade the children come
And took them in Your gentle arms and smiled,
Grant me unfailing patience through the days
To understand and help my little child.

I would not only give his body care
And guide his young dependent steps along
The wholesome ways, but I would know his heart,
Attuning mine to childhood's griefs and song.

Oh, give me vision to discern the child
Behind whatever he may do or say,
The wise humility to learn from him
The while I strive to teach him day by day.

ADELAIDE LOVE

The Reading Mother

I had a Mother who read to me
Sagas of pirates who scoured the sea,
Cutlasses clenched in their yellow teeth,
"Blackbirds" stowed in the hold beneath

I had a Mother who read me lays
Of ancient and gallant and golden days;
Stories of Marion and Ivanhoe,
Which every boy has a right to know.

I had a Mother who read me tales
Of Gelert the hound of the hills of Wales,
True to his trust till his tragic death,
Faithfulness blent with his final breath.

I had a Mother who read me the things
That wholesome life to the boy heart brings—
Stories that stir with an upward touch,
Oh, that each mother of boys were such!

You may have tangible wealth untold;
Caskets of jewels and coffers of gold.
Richer than I you can never be—
I had a Mother who read to me.

STRICKLAND GILLILAN

Washing the Dishes

When we on simple rations sup
How easy is the washing up!
But heavy feeding complicates
The task by soiling many plates.

And though I grant that I have prayed
That we might find a serving-maid,
I'd scullion all my days, I think,
To see Her smile across the sink!

I wash, she wipes. In water hot
I souse each dish and pan and pot;
While Taffy mutters, purrs, and begs,
And rubs himself against my legs.

The man who never in his life
Has washed the dishes with his wife
Or polished up the silver plate—
He still is largely celibate.

One warning: there is certain ware
That must be handled with all care:
The Lord Himself will give you up
If you should drop a willow cup!

CHRISTOPHER MORLEY

Building A Temple

Gone is the builder's temple,
Crumbled into the dust;
Low lies each stately pillar,
Food for consuming rust.
But the temple the teacher builded
Will last while the ages roll,
For that beautiful unseen temple
Is a child's immortal soul.

AUTHOR UNKNOWN

THE FORMATIVE PERIOD for building character for eternity is in the nursery. The mother is queen of that realm and sways a scepter more potent than that of kings or priests.

AUTHOR UNKNOWN

Mothers

the last time i was home
to see my mother we kissed
exchanged pleasantries
and unpleasantries pulled a warm
comforting silence around
us and read separate books

i remember the first time
i consciously saw her
we were living in a three room
apartment on burns avenue

mommy always sat in the dark
i don't know how i knew that but she did

that night i stumbled into the kitchen
maybe because i've always been
a night person or perhaps because i had wet
the bed
she was sitting on a chair
the room was bathed in moonlight diffused through
     tiny window panes
she may have been smoking but maybe not
her hair was three-quarters her height
which made me a strong believer in the samson myth
and very black

i'm sure i just hung there by the door
i remember thinking: what a beautiful lady
she was very deliberately waiting
perhaps for my father to come home
from his night job or maybe for a dream
that had promised to come by
"come here" she said "i'll teach you
a poem: *i see the moon*
       the moon sees me
       god bless the moon
       and god bless me"
i taught that to my son
who recited it for her
just to say we must learn
to bear the pleasures
as we have borne the pains

NIKKI GIOVANNI

Come, My Little Children

Come, my little children, here are songs for you;
Some are short and some are long, and all, all are new.
You must learn to sing them very small and clear,
Very true to time and tune and pleasing to the ear.

Mark the note that rises, mark the notes that fall,
Mark the time when broken, and the swing of it all.
So when the night is come, and you have gone to bed,
All the songs you love to sing shall echo in your head.

ROBERT LOUIS STEVENSON

I THINK, at a child's birth, if a mother could ask
a fairy godmother to endow it with the most
useful gift, that gift would be curiosity.

ELEANOR ROOSEVELT

The Hand that Rocks the Cradle

Blessing on the hand of women!
Angels guard its strength and grace,
In the palace, cottage, hovel,
Oh, no matter where the place;
Would that never storms assailed it,
Rainbows ever gently curled;
For the hand that rocks the cradle
Is the hand that rules the world.

Infancy's the tender fountain,
Power may with beauty flow,
Mother's first to guide the streamlets,
From them souls unresting grow—
Grow on for the good or evil,
Sunshine streamed or evil hurled;
For the hand that rocks the cradle
Is the hand that rules the world.

Woman, how divine your mission
Here upon our natal sod!
Keep, oh, keep the young heart open
Always to the breath of God!
All true trophies of the ages
Are from mother-love impearled;

For the hand that rocks the cradle
Is the hand that rules the world.

Blessings on the hand of women!
Fathers, sons, and daughters cry,
And the sacred song is mingled
With the worship in the sky—
Mingles where no tempest darkens,
Rainbows evermore are hurled;
For the hand that rocks the cradle
Is the hand that rules the world.

WILLIAM ROSS WALLACE

MY MOTHER said to me, "If you are a
soldier, you will become a general. If you
are a monk, you will become the Pope."
Instead I was a painter, and I became
Picasso.

PABLO PICASSO

The Blind Child

I know what mother's face is like,
Although I cannot see;
It's like the music of a bell;
It's like the roses I can smell—
Yes, these it's like to me.

I know what father's face is like;
I'm sure I know it all;
It's like his whistle on the air;
It's like his arms which take such care
And never let me fall.

And I can tell what God is like—
The God whom no one sees.
He's everything my parents seem;
He's fairer than my fondest dream,
And greater than all these.

AUTHOR UNKNOWN

The Bible

We search the world for truth. We cull
The good, the true, the beautiful,
From graven stone and written scroll.
And all old flower-fields of the soul:
And, weary seekers of the best.
We come back laden from our quest.
To find that all the sages said
Is in the Book our mothers read.

JOHN GREENLEAF WHITTIER

WOMEN know:
The way to rear up children (to be just).
They know a simple, merry, tender knack
Of tying sashes, fitting baby shoes,
And stringing pretty words that make no sense,
And kissing full sense into empty words.

ELIZABETH BARRETT BROWNING

ONE GOOD mother is worth a hundred schoolmasters.

GEORGE HERBERT

The Joy of Reading

As from the house your mother sees
You playing round the garden trees,
So you may see, if you will look
Through the windows of this book,
Another child, far, far away,
And in another garden, play.
But do not think you can at all,
By knocking on the window, call
That child to hear you. He intent
Is all on his play-business bent.
He does not hear, he will not look,
Nor yet be lured out of this book.
For, long ago, the truth to say,
He has grown up and gone away,
And it is but a child of air
That lingers in the garden there.

ROBERT LOUIS STEVENSON

Homework for Annabelle

$A = bh$ over 2.
    3.14 is π.
But I'd forgotten, if I ever knew,
    What R's divided by.
Though I knew once, I'd forgotten clean
What a girl must study to reach fifteen—
How V is Volume and M's for Mass,
And the hearts of the young are brittle as glass.

I had forgotten, and half with pride,
    Fifteen's no field of clover.
So here I sit at Annabelle's side,
    Learning my lessons over.
For help is something you have to give
When daughters are faced with the Ablative
Or first encounter in any school
Immutable gender's mortal rule.

Day after day for a weary spell,
    When the dusk has pitched its tents,
I sit with a book and Annabelle
    At the hour of confidence
And rummage for lore I had long consigned
To cobwebby attics of my mind,

Like: For the Radius, write down *R*,
The Volga's a river, Vega's a star,
Brazil's in the Tropic of Capricorn,
And heart is a burden that has to be borne.

Oh high is the price of parenthood,
    And daughters may cost you double.
You dare not forget, as you thought you could,
    That youth is a plague and trouble.
N times 7 is 7n—
Here I go learning it all again:
The climates of continents tend to vary,
The verb "to love"'s not auxiliary,
Tomorrow will come and today will pass,
But the hearts of the young are brittle as glass.

PHYLLIS MCGINLEY

Picture Books in Winter

Summer fading, winter comes—
Frosty mornings, tingling thumbs
Window robins, winter rooks,
And the picture story-books.

Water now is turned to stone
Nurse and I can walk upon;
Still we can find the flowing brooks
In the picture story-books.

All the pretty things put by
Wait upon the children's eye,
Sheep and shepherd, trees and crooks,
In the picture story-books.

We may see how all things are,
Seas and cities, near and far,
And the flying fairies' looks,
In the picture story-books.

How am I to sing your praise,
Happy chimney-corner days,
Sitting safe in nursery nooks,
Reading picture story-books?

ROBERT LOUIS STEVENSON

Social Studies

Woody says, "Let's *make* our soap,
It's easy.
We learned about it
In school."
He told Mother,
"All you do is
Take a barrel.
Bore holes in the sides,
And fill it with straw.
Ashes on top—"

"No," said Mother.

MARY NEVILLE

THE MOTHER's heart is the child's
schoolroom.

HENRY WARD BEECHER

The Minuet

Grandma told me all about it,
Told me so I couldn't doubt it,
How she danced, my grandma danced; long ago—
How she held her pretty head,
How her dainty skirt she spread,
How she slowly leaned and rose—long ago.

Grandma's hair was bright and sunny,
Dimpled cheeks, too, oh, how funny!
Really quite a pretty girl—long ago.
Bless her! Why she wears a cap,
Grandma does, and takes a nap
Every single day; and yet
Grandma danced the minuet—long ago.

"Modern ways are quite alarming,"
Grandma say, "but boys were charming"
(Girls and boys she means, of course) "long ago."
Brave but modest, grandly shy;
She would like to have us try
Just to feel like those who met
In the graceful minuet—long ago.

MARY MAPES DODGE

In An Iridescent Time

My mother, when young, scrubbed laundry
    in a tub,
She and her sisters on an old brick walk
Under the apple trees, sweet rub-a-dub.
The bees came round their heads, and wrens
    made talk.
Four young ladies each with a rainbow board
Honed their knuckles, wrung their wrists to red,
Tossed back their braids and wiped their
    aprons wet.
The Jersey calf beyond the back fence roared;
And all the soft day, swarms about their pet
Buzzed at his big brown eyes and bullish head.
Four times they rinsed, they said. Some things
    they starched,
Then shook them from the baskets two by two,
And pinned the fluttering intimacies of life
Between the lilac bushes and the yew:
Brown gingham, pink, and skirts of Alice blue.

RUTH STONE

Mutterings Over the Crib of a Deaf Child

"How will he hear the bell at school
Arrange the broken afternoon,
And know to run across the cool
Grasses where the starlings cry,
Or understand the day is gone?"

Well, someone lifting curious brows
Will take the measure of the clock.
And he will see the birchen boughs
Outside sagging dark from the sky,
And the shade crawling upon the rock.

"And how will he know to rise at morning?
His mother has other sons to waken,
She has the stove she must build to burning
Before the coals of the nighttime die;
And he never stirs when he is shaken."

I take it the air affects the skin,
And you remember, when you were young,
Sometimes you could feel the dawn begin,
And the fire would call you, by and by,
Out of bed and bring you along.

"Well, good enough. To serve his needs
All kinds of arrangements can be made.
But what you will do if his finger bleeds?
Or a bobwhite whistles invisibly
And flutes like an angel off in the shade?"

He will learn pain. And, as for the bird,
It is always darkening when that comes out.
I will putter as though I had not heard,
And lift him into my arms and sing
Whether he hears my song or not.

JAMES WRIGHT

MY MOTHER was the most beautiful woman
I ever saw. All I am I owe to my mother.
I attribute all my success in life to the moral,
intellectual, and physical education I received
from my mother.

GEORGE WASHINGTON

THE MOTHERS of sons work from son-up to son-down.

AUTHOR UNKNOWN

A Child's Evening Prayer

Ere on my bed my limbs I lay,
God grant me grace my prayers to say;
O God! Preserve my mother dear
In strength and health for many a year;
And, O! Preserve my father too
And may I pay him reverence due;
And may I my best thoughts employ
To be my parents' hope and joy;
And O! Preserve my brothers both
From evil doings and from sloth,
And may we always love each other
Our friends, our father, and our mother;
And still, O Lord, to me impart
An innocent and grateful heart,
That after my last sleep I may
Awake to thy eternal day! Amen.

SAMUEL TAYLOR COLERIDGE

Praising

No one in the world can take
the place of your mother.
Right or wrong, from her viewpoint
you are always right.

HARRY TRUMAN

A MOTHER is one to whom you hurry
when you are troubled.

EMILY DICKINSON

Mother's Love

Her love is like an island
In life's ocean, vast and wide,
A peaceful, quiet shelter
From the wind and rain, and tide.

'Tis bound on the north by Hope.
By Patience on the west,
By tender Counsel on the south,
And on the east by Rest.

Above it like a beacon light
Shine faith, and truth, and prayer;
And through the changing scenes of life,
I find a haven there.

AUTHOR UNKNOWN

I Will Make You Brooches

I will make you brooches and toys for your delight,
Of bird-song at morning and star-shine at night.
I will build a palace fit for you and me,
Of green days in forests and blue days at sea.

I will make my kitchen, and you shall keep your room,
Where white flows the river and bright blows the broom,
And you shall wash your linen and keep your body white
In rainfall at morning and dewfall at night.

And this shall be for music when no one else is near,
The fine song for singing, the rare song to hear!
That only I remember, that only you admire,
Of the broad road that stretches and the roadside fire.

ROBERT LOUIS STEVENSON

EVERY beetle is a gazelle in the eye of its mother.

MOORISH PROVERB

The Woman Who Understands

Somewhere she waits to make you win, your soul
*   in her firm, white hands—*
Somewhere God has made for you, the Woman
*   Who Understands!*

As the tide went out she found him
        Lashed to a spar of Despair,
The wreck of his Ship around him—
        The wreck of his Dreams in the air;
Found him and loved him and gathered
        The soul of him close to her heart—
The soul that had sailed an uncharted sea,
The soul that had sought to win and be free—
        The soul of which she was part!
                And there in the dusk she cried to the man,
                "Win your battle—you can, you can!"

Broken by Fate, unrelenting,
        Scarred by the lashings of Chance;
Bitter his heart—unrepenting—
        Hardened by Circumstance;
Shadowed by Failure ever,
        Cursing, he would have died,

But the touch of her hand, her strong warm hand,
And her love of his soul, took full command,
    Just at the turn of the tide!
      Standing beside him, filled with trust,
    "Win!" she whispered, "you must, you must!"

Helping and loving and guiding,
    Urging when that were best,
Holding her fears in hiding
    Deep in her quiet breast;
This is the woman who kept him
    True to his standards lost,
When tossed in the storm and stress of strife,
He thought himself through with the game of life
    And ready to pay the cost.
      Watching and guarding, whispering still,
    "Win you can—and you will, you will."

This is the story of ages
    This is the Woman's way;
Wiser than seers or sages,
    Lifting us day by day;
Facing all things with a courage
    Nothing can daunt or dim,
      Treading Life's path, wherever it leads—

Lined with flowers or choked with weeds,
But ever with him—with him!
Guidon—comrade—golden spur—
The men who win are helped by her!

Somewhere she waits, strong in belief, your
Soul in her firm, white hands:
Thank well your God, when she comes to you,
The Woman Who Understands!

EVERARD JACK APPLETON

WOMEN are aristocrats, and it is always
the mother who makes us feel that we belong
to the better sort.

JOHN LANCASTER SPALDING

A MOTHER'S heart is a patchwork of love.

AUTHOR UNKNOWN

Mother

As long ago we carried to your knees
    The tales and treasures of eventful days,
    Knowing no deed too humble for your praise,
Nor any gift too trivial to please,

So still we bring with older smiles and tears,
    What gifts we may to claim the old, dear right;
    Your faith beyond the silence and the night;
Your love still close and watching through the years.

AUTHOR UNKNOWN

THE MOMENT a child is born, the mother
is also born. She never existed before.
The woman existed, but the mother, never.
A mother is something absolutely new.

RAJINEESH

Apology for Youth

Stand at my window;
watch them pass;
a lass and a lad,
a lad and a lass.

This is a way
to go to school,
learning an olden,
golden rule.

They seek for wisdom
in a book;
then they look up
and look—and look.

And wonder, wonder
if, after all,
wisdom is so
reciprocal.

They ask for beauty,
ask for truth
who have no thought
to ask for youth.

Theirs are the earth,
the sea, the sky;
they sing; they dance,
they float; they fly.

Why do they hurry,
hurry so?
Can they or will they
or do they know

They will earn some love;
they will learn some truth,
but never learn
nor earn back youth.

Stand at my window,
lad and lass;
let not this youth,
this young love pass.

Hold the wonder;
love the lore
you would one day change
the slow years for.

SISTER M. MADELEVA, C.S.C.

If...

If I could give you diamonds
For each tear you cried for me;
If I could give you sapphires
For each truth you helped me see.

If I could give you rubies
For the heartache that you've known;
If I could give you pearls
For the wisdom that you've shown;
You'd have a treasure, Mother,
That would mount up to the skies,
That would almost match the sparkle
In your kind and loving eyes.

But I have no pearls, no diamonds,
As I'm sure you're well aware,
So I'll give you gifts more precious,
Devotion, love, and care.

AUTHOR UNKNOWN

Nobility

True worth is in *being* not *seeming*,—
In doing, each day that goes by,
Some little good—not in dreaming
Of great things to do by and by.

For whatever men say in their blindness,
And in spite of the fancies of youth,
There's nothing so kingly as kindness,
And nothing so royal as truth.

We cannot make bargains for blisses,
Nor catch them like fishes in nets;
And sometimes the thing our life misses
Helps more than the thing which it gets.

For good lieth not in pursuing,
Not gaining of great nor of small,
But just in the doing, and doing
As we would be done by, is all.

ALICE CARY

Nancy Hanks

If Nancy Hanks
Came back as a ghost,
Seeking news
Of what she loved most,
She'd ask first,
"Where's my son?
What's happened to Abe?
What's he done?
"Poor little Abe,
Left all alone
Except for Tom,
Who's a rolling stone;
He was only nine
The year I died.
I remember still
How hard he cried.

"Scraping along
In a little shack
With hardly a shirt
To cover his back,
And a prairie wind
To blow him down,
Or pinching times
If he went to town.

"You wouldn't know
About my son?
Did he grow tall?
Did he have fun?
Did he learn to read?
Did he get to town?
Do you know his name?
Did he get on?"

ROSEMARY BENET

ONE LAMP, thy mother's love
amid the stars, shall lift its pure
flame changeless, and before
the throne of God, burn through
eternity—Holy—as it was lit
and lent thee here.

NATHANIEL PARKER WILLIS

God Give Me Joy

God give me joy in the common things:
In the dawn that lures, the eve that sings.

In the new grass sparkling after rain,
In the late wind's wild and weird refrain;

In the springtime's spacious field of gold,
In the precious light by winter doled.

God give me joy in the love of friends,
In their dear home talk as summer ends;

In the songs of children, unrestrained;
In the sober wisdom age has gained.

God give me joy in the tasks that press,
In the memories that burn and bless;

In the thought that life has love to spend,
In the faith that God's at journey's end.

God give me hope for each day that springs,
God give me joy in the common things!

THOMAS CURTIS CLARK

A Mother's Love

There are times when only a Mother
Can understand our tears,
Can soothe our disappointments
And quiet all our fears.

There are times when only a Mother
Can share the joy we feel;
When something that we've dreamed about
Quite suddenly is real.

There are times when only a Mother's faith
Can help us on life's way,
And inspire in us the confidence
We need from day to day.

A Mother's heart, a Mother's faith,
A Mother's steadfast love,
Were fashioned by the Angels
And sent from God above.

AUTHOR UNKNOWN

Forgiving

The heart of a mother is
a deep abyss at the bottom
of which you will always
find forgiveness.

HONORE DE BALZAC

Easily Given

It was only a sunny smile,
    And little it cost in the giving;
        But it scattered the night
        Like morning light,
    And made the day worth living.
Through life's dull warp a woof it wove,
In shining colors of light and love,
And the angels smiled as they watched above,
    Yet little it cost in giving.

It was only a kindly word,
    And a word that was lightly spoken;
        Yet not in vain,
        For it stilled the pain
    Of a heart that was nearly broken.
It strengthened a fate beset by fears
And groping blindly through mists of tears
For light to brighten the coming years,
    Although it was lightly spoken.

It was only a helping hand,
    And it seemed of little availing;
        But its clasps were warm,
        And it saved from harm
    A brother whose strength was failing.

Its touch was tender as angels' wings,
But it rolled the stone from the hidden springs,
And pointed the way to higher things,
    Though it seemed of little availing.

A smile, a word, a touch,
    And each is easily given;
        Yet one may win
        A soul from sin
    Or smooth the way to heaven.
A smile may lighten a falling heart,
A word may soften pain's keenest smart,
A touch may lead us from sin apart—
    How easily each is given!

AUTHOR UNKNOWN

THE REAL RELIGION of the world comes
from women much more than from men—
from mothers most of all, who carry
the key of our souls in the bosom.

OLIVER WENDELL HOLMES

Rock Me to Sleep

Backward, turn backward, O Time, in your flight,
Make me a child again just for to-night!
Mother, come back from the echoless shore,
Take me again to your heart as of yore;
Kiss from my forehead the furrows of care,
Smooth the few silver threads out of my hair;
Over my slumbers your loving watch keep—
Rock me to sleep, mother—rock me to sleep!

Backward, flow backward, O tide of the years!
I am so weary of toil and of tears—
Toil without recompense, tears all in vain—
Take them and give me my childhood again!
I have grown weary of dust and decay,
Weary of flinging my soul-wealth away,
Weary of sowing for others to reap—
Rock me to sleep, mother—rock me to sleep!

Tired of the hollow, the base, the untrue,
Mother, O mother, my heart calls for you!
Many a summer the grass has grown green,
Blossomed and faded, our faces between;
Yet, with strong yearning and passionate pain,
Long I to-night for your presence again;
Come from the silence so long and so deep—
Rock me to sleep, mother—rock me to sleep!

Over my heart in the days that are flown,
No love like mother-love ever has shone;
No other worship abides and endures,
Faithful, unselfish, and patient, like yours;
None like a mother can charm away pain
From the sick soul and the world-weary brain;
Slumber's soft calm o'er my heavy lids creep—
Rock me to sleep, mother—rock me to sleep!

Come, let your brown hair, just lighted with gold,
Fall on your shoulders again as of old;
Let it drop over my forehead to-night,
Shading my faint eyes away from the light;
For with its sunny-edge shadows once more,
Haply will throng the sweet vision of yore;
Lovingly, softly, its bright billows sweep—
Rock me to sleep, mother—rock me to sleep!

Mother, dear mother, the years have been long
Since I last listened your lullaby song;
Sing then, and unto my soul it shall seem
Womanhood's years have been only a dream.
Clasped to your heart in a loving embrace,
With your light lashes just sweeping my face,
Never hereafter to wake or to weep—
Rock me to sleep, mother—rock me to sleep!

ELIZABETH AKERS

Mother O' Mine

If I were hanged on the highest hill,
Mother o' mine, O mother o' mine!
I know whose love would follow me still,
Mother o' mine, O mother o' mine!

If I were drowned in the deepest sea,
Mother o' mine, O mother o' mine!
I know whose tears would come down to me,
Mother o' mine, O mother o' mine!

If I were damned of body and soul,
I know whose prayers would make me whole,
Mother o' mine, O mother o' mine!

RUDYARD KIPLING

SHE MAY SCOLD you for the little things,
but never for the big ones.

HARRY TRUMAN

WHATEVER is unsure in this stinking dunghill
of a world, a mother's love is not.

JAMES JOYCE

Mercy

The quality of mercy is not strained;
It droppeth as the gentle rain from heaven
Upon the place beneath; it is twice blest,—
It blesseth him that gives and him that takes;
'Tis mightiest in the mightiest; it becomes
The throned monarch better than his crown;
His scepter shows the force of temporal power,
The attribute to awe and majesty,
Wherein doth sit the dread and fear of kings.

But mercy is above this sceptred sway,—
It is enthroned in the heart of kings,
It is an attribute of God himself;
And earthly power doth then show likest God's,
When mercy seasons justice.

WILLIAM SHAKESPEARE

Life Lessons

I learn, as the years roll onward
    And leave the past behind,
That much I had counted sorrow
    But proves that God is kind;
That many a flower I had longed for
    Had hidden a thorn of pain,
And many a rugged bypath
    Led to fields of ripened grain.

The clouds that cover the sunshine
    They can not banish the sun;
And the earth shines out the brighter
    When the weary rain is done.
We must stand in the deepest shadow
    To see the clearest light;
And often through wrong's own darkness
    Comes the very strength of light.

The sweetest rest is at even,
    After a wearisome day,
When the heavy burden of labor
    Has borne from our hearts away;
And those who have never known sorrow
    Can not know the infinite peace

That falls on the troubled spirit
    When it sees at least release.

We must live through the dreary winter
    If we would value the spring;
And the woods must be cold and silent
    Before the robins sing.
The flowers must be buried in darkness
    Before they can bud and bloom,
And the sweetest, warmest sunshine
    Comes after the storm and gloom.

AUTHOR UNKNOWN

MOTHER is the name for God in the lips
and hearts of little children.

WILLIAM MAKEPEACE THACKERAY

THE SWEETEST sounds to mortals given are
heard in Mother, Home and Heaven.

WILLIAM GOLDSMITH BROWN

There Is Nothing False in Thee

There is nothing false in thee.
In thy heat the youngest body
Has warmth and light.
In thee the quills of the sun
Find adornment.
What does not die
Is with thee.

Thou art clothed in robes of music.
Thy voice awakens wings.

And still more with thee
Are the flowers of earth made bright.

Upon thy deeps the fiery sails
Of heaven glide.

Thou art the radiance and the joy.
Thy heart shall only fail
When all else has fallen.

What does not perish
Lives in thee.

KENNETH PATCHEN

MY MOTHER had a great deal of trouble with me, but I think she enjoyed it.

MARK TWAIN

To Make This Life Worth While

May every soul that touches mine—
Be it the slightest contact—
Get therefrom some good;
Some little grace; one kindly thought;
One aspiration yet unfelt;
One bit of courage
For the darkening sky;
One gleam of faith
To brave the thickening ills of life;
One glimpse of brighter skies
Beyond the gathering mists—
To make this life worth while...

GEORGE ELIOT

MOTHER—that was the bank where we deposited all our hurts and worries.

T. DEWITT TALMAGE

My Mother's Garden

Her heart is like her garden,
Old-fashioned, quaint and sweet,
With here a wealth of blossoms,
And there a still retreat.
Sweet violets are hiding,
We know as we pass by,
And lilies, pure as angel thoughts,
Are opening somewhere nigh.

Forget-me-nots there linger,
to full perfection brought,
And there bloom purple pansies
In many a tender thought.
There love's own roses blossom,
As from enchanted ground,
And lavish perfume exquisite
The whole glad year around.

And in that quiet garden—
The garden of her heart—
Songbirds are always singing
Their songs of cheer apart.

And from it floats forever,
O'ercoming sin and strife,
Sweet as the breath of roses blown,
The fragrance of her life.

ALICE E. ALLEN

A MOTHER is the truest friend we have.
When trials heavy and sudden fall upon
us; when adversity takes the place of
prosperity; when friends who rejoice
with us in our sunshine desert us; when
trouble thickens around us, still will she
cling to us, and endeavor by her kind
precepts and counsels to dissipate the
clouds of darkness and cause peace
to return to our hearts.

WASHINGTON IRVING

Letting Go

I remember my mother' prayers
and they have followed me.
The have clung to me all my life.

ABRAHAM LINCOLN

I Remember, I Remember

I remember, I remember,
The house where I was born,
The little window where the sun
Came peeping in at morn;
He never came a wink too soon,
Nor brought too long a day,
But now, I often wish the night
Had borne my breath away!

I remember, I remember,
The roses, red and white,
The violets, and the lily-cups,
Those flowers made of light!
The lilacs where the robin built,
And where my brother set
The laburnum on his birthday,—
The tree is living yet!

THOMAS HOOD

This Little Gift

Before this little girl was come
The little owner had made haste for home;
And from the door of where the eternal dwell,
Looked back on human beings and smiled farewell.

O may this grief remain the only one!
O may our house be still a garrison
Of smiling children, and for evermore
The tune of little feet be heard along the floor!

ROBERT LOUIS STEVENSON

THE MOTHER-CHILD relationship is paradoxical
and, in a sense, tragic. It requires the most
intense love on the mother's side, yet this very
love must help the child grow away from the
mother, and to become fully independent.

ERIC FROMM

Birches

When I see birches bend left to right
Across the line of straighter darker trees,
I like to think some boy's been swinging them
But swinging doesn't bend them down to stay.
Ice-storms do that. Often you must have seen them
Loaded with ice a sunny winter morning
After a rain. They click upon themselves
As the breeze rises, and turn many-colored
As the stir cracks and crazes their enamel.
Soon the sun's warmth makes them shed crystals shells
Shattering and avalanching on the snow-crust—
Such heaps of broken glass to sweep away
You'd think the inner dome of heaven had fallen.
They are dragged to the withered bracken by the load,
And they seem not to break; though once they are bowed
So low for so long, they never right themselves:
You may see their trunks arching in the woods
Years afterwards, trailing their leaves on the ground
Like girls on hands and knees that throw their hair
Before them over their heads to dry in the sun.
But I was going to say when Truth broke in
With all her matter-of-fact about the ice-storm
I should prefer to have some boy bend them
As he went out and in to fetch the cows—

Some boy too far from town to learn baseball,
Whose only play was what he found himself,
Summer or winter, and could play alone.
One by one he subdued his father's trees
By riding them down over and over again
Until he took the stiffness out of them,
And not one but hung limp, not one was left
For him to conquer. He learned all there was
To learn about not launching out too soon
And so not carrying the tree away
Clear to the ground. He always kept his poise
To the top branches, climbing carefully
With the same pains you use to fill a cup
Up to the brim, and even above the brim.
Then he flung outward, feet first, with a swish,
Kicking his way down through the air to the ground.
So was I once myself a swinger of birches.
And so I dream of going back to be.
It's when I'm weary of considerations,
And life is too much like a pathless wood
Where your face burns and tickles with the cobwebs
Broken across it, and one eye is weeping
From a twig's having lashed across it open.
I'd like to get away from earth awhile
And then come back to it and begin over.

May no fate willfully misunderstand me
And half grant what I wish and snatch me away
Not to return. Earth's the right place for love:
I don't know where' it's likely to go better.
I'd like to go by climbing a birch tree,
And climb black branches up a snow-white trunk
Toward heaven, till the trees could bear no more,
But dipped its top and set me down again.
That would be good both going and coming back.
One could do worse than be a swinger of birches.

ROBERT FROST

HE IS a poor son whose sonship does not
make him desire to serve all men's mothers.

HENRY EMERSON FOSDICK

A Prayer for a Little Home

God send us a little home
To come back to when we roam—
Low walls and fluted tiles,
Wide windows, a view for miles;
Red firelight and deep chairs;
Small white beds upstairs;
Great talk in little nooks;
Dim colors, rows of books;
One picture on each wall;
Not many things at all.

God send us a little ground—
Tall trees standing round,
Homely flowers in brown sod,
Overhead, the stars, O God!
God bless, when winds blow,
Our home and all we know.

FLORENCE BONE

Speak Out

If you have a friend worth loving,
    Love him. Yes, and let him know
That you love him, ere life's evening
    Tinge his brow with sunset glow.
Why should good words ne'er be said
Of a friend—till he is dead?

If you hear a song that thrills you,
    Sung by any child of song,
Praise it. Do not let the singer
    Wait deserved praises long.
Why should one who thrills your heart
Lack the joy you may impart?

If you hear a prayer that moves you
    By its humble, pleading tone,
Join it. Do not let the seeker
    Bow before his God alone.
Why should not thy brother share
The strength of "two or three" in prayer?

If your work is made more easy
    By a friendly, helping hand,
Say so. Speak out brave and truly,
    Ere the darkness veil the land.

Should a brother workman dear
Falter for a word of cheer?

Scatter thus your seeds of kindness
        All enriching as you go—
Leave them. Trust the Harvest-Giver;
        He will make each seed to grow.

So, until the happy end,
Your life shall never lack a friend.

AUTHOR UNKNOWN

A MOTHER takes twenty years
to make a man of her boy,
and another woman makes
a fool of him in twenty minutes.

ROBERT FROST

My Early Home

Here sparrows build upon the trees,
    And stock-dove hides her nest;
The leaves are winnowed by the breeze
    Into a calmer rest:
The blackcap's song was very sweet,
    That used the rose to kiss;
It made the paradise complete:
    My early home was this.

The redbreast from the sweetbrier bush
    Dropt down to pick the worm;
On the horse-chestnut sang the thrush,
    O'er the house where I was born;
The moonlight, like a shower of pearls,
    Felt o'er this "bower of bliss,"
And on the bench sat boys and girls:
    My early home was this.

The old house stooped just like a cave,
    Thatched o'er with mosses green;
Winter around the walls would rave,
    But all was calm within;

The trees are here all green agen,
    Here bees and flowers still kiss,
But flowers and trees seemed sweeter then:
My early home was this.

JOHN CLARE

THOU ART thy mother's glass,
and she in thee calls back
the lovely April of her prime.

WILLIAM SHAKESPEARE

Ballade of Lost Objects

Where are the ribbons I tie my hair with?
    Where is my lipstick? Where are my hose—
The sheer ones hoarded these weeks to wear with
    Frocks the closets do not disclose?
Perfumes, petticoats, sports chapeaux,
    The blouse Parisian, the earring Spanish—
Everything suddenly ups and goes.
    And where in the world did the children vanish?

This is the house I used to share with
    Girls in pinafores, shier than does.
I can recall how they climbed my stair with
    Gales of giggles, on their tiptoes.
Last seen wearing both braids and bows
    (But looking rather Raggedy-Annish),
When they departed nobody knows—
    Where in the world did the children vanish?

Two tall strangers, now, I must bear with,
    Decked in my personal furbelows,
Raiding the larder, rending the air with
    Gossip and terrible radios.
Neither my friends nor quite my foes,
    Alien, beautiful, stern, and clannish,

Here they dwell, while the wonder grows:
    Where in the world did the children vanish?

Prince, I warn you, under the rose,
    Time is the thief you cannot banish.
These are my daughters, I suppose.
    But where in the world did the children vanish?

PHYLLIS McGINLEY

MOTHER, the ribbons of your love are woven
around my heart.

AUTHOR UNKNOWN

When I Have Time

When I have time so many things I'll do
To make life happier and more fair
For those whose lives are crowded now with care;
I'll help to lift them from their low despair
    When I have time.

When I have time the friend I love so well
Shall know no more these weary, toiling days;
I'll lead her feet in pleasant paths always
And cheer her heart with words of sweetest praise,
    When I have time.

When you have time! The friend you hold so dear
May be beyond the reach of all your sweet intent;
May never know that you so kindly meant
To fill her life with sweet content
    When you had time.

Now is the time! Ah, friend, no longer wait
To scatter loving smiles and words of cheer
To those around whose lives are now so drear;
They may not need you in the coming year—
    Now is the time!

AUTHOR UNKNOWN

The Road Not Taken

Two roads diverged in a yellow wood,
And sorry I could not travel both
And be one traveler, long I stood
And looked down one as far as I could
To where it bent in the undergrowth;

Then took the other, just as fair,
And having perhaps the better claim,
Because it was grassy and wanted wear;
Though as for that the passing there
Had worn them really about the same,

And both that morning equally lay
In leaves no step had trodden black.
Oh, I kept the first for another day!
Yet knowing how way leads on to way,
I doubted if I should ever come back.

I shall be telling this with a sigh
Somewhere ages and ages hence:
Two roads diverged in a wood, and I—
I took the one less traveled by,
And that has made all the difference.

ROBERT FROST

Little Boy Blue

The little toy dog is covered with dust,
 But sturdy and stanch he stands;
And the little toy soldier is red with rust,
 And his musket molds in his hands.

Time was when the little toy dog was new,
 And the soldier was passing fair,
And that was the time when our Little Boy Blue
 Kissed them and put them there.

"Now don't you go till I come," he said,
 "And don't you make any noise!"
So toddling off to his trundle-bed
 He dreamt of the pretty toys.

And as he was dreaming, an angel song
 Awakened our Little Boy Blue—
Oh, the years are many, the years are long,
 But the little toy friends are true!

Ay, faithful to Little Boy Blue they stand,
 Each in the same old place,
Awaiting the touch of a little hand,
 The smile of a little face.

And they wonder, as waiting these long years through,
    In the dust of that little chair,
What has become of our Little Boy Blue
    Since he kissed them and put them there.

EUGENE FIELD

A MOTHER'S happiness is like a beacon,
lighting up the future but reflected also
on the past in the guise of fond memories.

HONORE DE BALZAC

You...

You filled my days with rainbow lights,
Fairy tales and sweet dream nights,
A kiss to wipe away my tears,
Gingerbread to ease my fears.
You gave the gift of life to me
And then in love you set me free.

I thank you for your tender care,
For deep, warm hugs and being there.
I hope that when you think of me,
A part of you you'll always see.

AUTHOR UNKNOWN

MIRROR, mirror on the wall,
I am my mother after all.

AUTHOR UNKNOWN

To My Son

I will not say to you, "This is the way; walk in it."
For I do not know your way or where the Spirit
     may call you.
It may be to paths I have never trod or ships on
     the sea leading to unimagined lands afar,
Or haply, to a star!
Or yet again
Through dark and perilous places racked with pain
     and full of fear
Your road may lead you far away from me or near—
I cannot guess or guide, but only stand aside.
Just this I say:
I know for every truth there is a way for each to
     walk, a right for each to choose, a truth to use.
And though you wander far, your soul will know
     that true path when you find it.
Therefore, go!
I will fear nothing for you day or night!
I will not grieve at all because your light is called
     by some new name;
Truth is the same!
It matters nothing to call it star or sun—
All light is one.

AUTHOR UNKNOWN

Everlasting Love

The tie which links mother
and child is of such pure
and immediate strength
as to never be violated.

WASHINGTON IRVING

A Prayer for a Mother's Birthday

Lord Jesus, Thou hast known
A Mother's love and tender care;
And Thou wilt hear, while for my own
Mother most dear I make this birthday prayer.

Protect her life, I pray,
Who gave the gift of life to me;
And may she know, from day to day,
The deepening glow of Life that comes from Thee.

As once upon her breast
Fearless and well content I lay,
So let her heart, on Thee at rest,
Feel fears depart and troubles fade away.

Her every wish fulfill;
And even if thou must refuse
In anything, let Thy wise will
A comfort bring such as kind mothers use.

Ah, hold her by the hand,
As once her hand held mine;
And though she may not understand
Life's winding way, lead her in peace divine.

I cannot pay my debt
For all the love that she has given;
But Thou, love's Lord, will not forget
Her due reward—bless her in earth and heaven.

HENRY VAN DYKE

ALL THAT I AM or ever hope to be,
I owe to my angel Mother.

ABRAHAM LINCOLN

MOTHER'S LOVE is peace.
It need not be acquired,
it need not be deserved.

ERICH FROMM

Mis' Smith

All day she hurried to get through
The same as lots of wimmin do;
Sometimes at night her husban' said,
"Ma, ain't you goin' to come to bed?"
And then she'd kinder give a hitch,
And pause half-way between a stitch,
And sorter sigh, and say that she
    Was ready as she'd ever be,
        She reckoned.

And so the years went one by one,
An' somehow she was never done;
An' when the angel said, as how
"Mis' Smith, it's time you rested now,"
She sorter raised her eyes to look
A second, as a stitch she took;
"All right, I'm comin' now," she says,
    "I'm ready as I'll ever be,
        I reckon."

ALBERT BIGELOW PAINE

Autumn (To My Mother)

How memory cuts away the years,
And how clean the picture comes
Of autumn days, brisk and busy;
Charged with keen sunshine.
And you, stirred with activity,
The spirit of those energetic days.

There was our back-yard,
So plain and stripped of green,
With even the weeds carefully pulled away
From the crooked red bricks that made the walk,
And the earth on either side so black.

Autumn and dead leaves burning in the sharp air.
And winter comforts coming in like a pageant.
I shall not forget them:—
Great jars laden with the raw green of pickles,
Standing in a solemn row across the back of the porch,
Exhaling the pungent dill;
And in the very centre of the yard,
You, tending the great catsup kettle of gleaming copper,
Where fat, red tomatoes bobbed up and down
Like jolly monks in a drunken dance.
And there were bland banks of cabbages that came by
the wagon-load,

Soon to be cut into delicate ribbons
Only to be crushed by the heavy, wooden stompers.
Such feathery whiteness—to come to kraut!
And after, there were grapes that hid their brightness
under a grey dust,
Then gushed thrilling, purple blood over the fire;
And enamelled crab-apples that tricked with their
fragrance
But were bitter to taste.
And there were spicy plums and ill-shaped quinces,
And long string beans floating in pans of clear water
Like slim, green fishes.
And there was fish itself,
Salted, silver herring from the city....

And you moved among these mysteries,
Absorbed and smiling and sure;
Stirring, tasting, measuring,
With the precision of a ritual.
I like to think of you in your years of power—
You, now, so shaken and so powerless—
High priestess of your home.

JEAN STARR UNTERMEYER

A **FATHER** may turn his back on his child, brother and sisters may become inveterate enemies, husbands may desert their wives, wives their husbands. But a mother's love endures through all.

WASHINGTON IRVING

Remembrance

This memory of my mother stays with me
   Throughout the years: the way she used to stand
   Framed in the door when any of her band
Of children left . . . as long as she could see
Their forms, she gazed, as if she seemed to be
   Trying to guard—to meet some far demand;
   And then before she turned to tasks at hand,
She breathed a little prayer inaudibly.

And now, I think, in some far heavenly place,
   She watches still, and yet is not distressed,
But rather as one who, after life's long race,
   Has found contentment in a well-earned rest,
There, in a peaceful, dreamlike reverie,
She waits, from earthly cares forever free.

MARGARET E. BRUNER

YOUTH FADES; love droops;
the leaves of friendship fall;
a mother's secret hope outlives them all.

OLIVER WENDELL HOLMES

When You Are Old

When you are old and gray and full of sleep
And nodding by the fire, take down this book,
And slowly read, and dream of the soft look
Your eyes had once, and of their shadows deep;

How many loved your moments of glad grace,
And loved your beauty with love false or true;
But one man loved the pilgrim soul in you,
And loved the sorrows of your changing face.

And bending down beside the glowing bars,
Murmur, a little sadly, how love fled
And paced upon the mountains overhead,
And hid his face amid a crowd of stars.

WILLIAM BUTLER YEATS

Love Is

Some people forget that love is
tucking you in and kissing you "Good night"
no matter how young or old you are

Some people don't remember that love is
listening and laughing and asking questions
no matter what your age

Few recognize that love is
commitment   responsibility   no fun at all
unless

Love is
You and me

NIKKI GIOVANNI

MOST OF ALL the other beautiful things in
life come by twos and threes, by dozens and
hundreds. Plenty of roses, stars, sunsets,
rainbows, brother and sisters, aunt and cousins,
comrades and friends . . . but only one mother
in the whole world.

KATE DOUGLAS WIGGEN

Somebody's Mother

The woman was old and ragged and gray
And bent with the chill of the Winter's day.

The street was wet with a recent snow
And the woman's feet were aged and slow.

She stood at the crossing and waited long,
Alone, uncared for, amid the throng

Of human beings who passed her by
Nor heeded the glance of her anxious eye.

Down the street, with laughter and shout,
Glad in the freedom of "school let out,"

Came the boys like a flock of sheep,
Hailing the snow piled white and deep.

Past the woman so old and gray
Hastened the children on their way.

Nor offered a helping hand to her—
So meek, so timid, afraid to stir

Lest the carriage wheels or the horses' feet
Should crowd her down in the slippery street.

At last came one of the merry troop,
The gayest laddie of all the group;

He paused beside her and whispered low,
"I'll help you cross, if you wish to go."

Her aged hand on his strong young arm
She placed, and so, without hurt or harm,

He guided the trembling feet along,
Proud that his own were firm and strong.

Then back again to his friends he went,
His young heart happy and well content.

"She's somebody's mother, boys, you know,
For all she's aged and poor and slow,

"And I hope some fellow will lend a hand
To help my mother, you understand,

"If ever she's poor and old and gray,
When her own dear boy is far away."

And "somebody's mother" bowed low her head
In her home that night, and the prayer she said

Was, "God be kind to the noble boy,
Who is somebody's son, and pride and joy!"

MARY DOW BRINE

Apologia

When I and the world
Were greener and fitter,
Many a bitter
Stone I hurled.
Many a curse
I used to pitch
At the universe,
Being so rich
I had goods to spare;
Could afford to notice
The blight on the lotus,
The worm in the pear.

But needier grown
(If little wiser)
Now, like a miser,
All that I own
I celebrate
Shamefacedly—
The pear on my plate,
The fruit on my tree,
Though sour and small;
Give, willy-nilly,
Thanks for the lily,
Spot and all.

PHYLLIS MCGINLEY

BECAUSE I feel that in the heavens above,
the angels, whispering one to another,
can find among their burning tears of love
none so devotional as that of "Mother,"
therefore by that dear name I have long
called you, you who are more than mother
unto me.

EDGAR ALLAN POE

A Wonderful Mother

God made a wonderful mother,
A mother who never grows old;
He made her smile of the sunshine,
And He molded her heart of pure gold;
In her eyes He placed bright shining stars,
In her cheeks, fair roses you see;
God made a wonderful mother,
And He gave that dear mother to me.

PAT O'REILLY

A MAN LOVES his sweetheart the most, his
wife the best, but his mother the longest.

IRISH PROVERB

Acknowledgments

Rosemary Benet. " Nancy Hanks " by Rosemary Carr Benet from *A Book of Americans* by Rosemary and Stephen Vincent Benet, Henry Holt & Company, © 1933 by Rosemary and Stephen Vincent Benet copyright renewed © 1961 by Rosemary Carr Benet. Reprinted with the permission of Brandt & Hochman Literary Agents, Inc. All rights reserved.

Nikki Giovanni. "Love Is " and "Mothers" by Nikki Giovanni from *Love Poems* by Nikki Giovanni © 1997. Reprinted with the permission of the author.

Edgar A. Guest. "Becoming A Dad" by Edgar A. Guest from *Collected Verse of Edgar A. Guest* © 1934 by The Reilly & Lee Co. Reprinted with permission of McGraw Hill Education.

Sister M. Madeleva CSC. "Apology for Youth" by Sister M. Madeleva from *The Last Four Things* by Sister M. Madeleva. Reprinted with the permission of The Congregation of the Sisters of the Holy Cross.

Phyllis McGinley. "Apologia" by Phyllis McGinley © 1954 by Phyllis McGinley copyright renewed © 1982 by Patricia Hayden Blake. First appeared in *Love Letters of Phyllis McGinley* published by The Viking Press. Reprinted with the permission of Curtis Brown Ltd.

Contributors